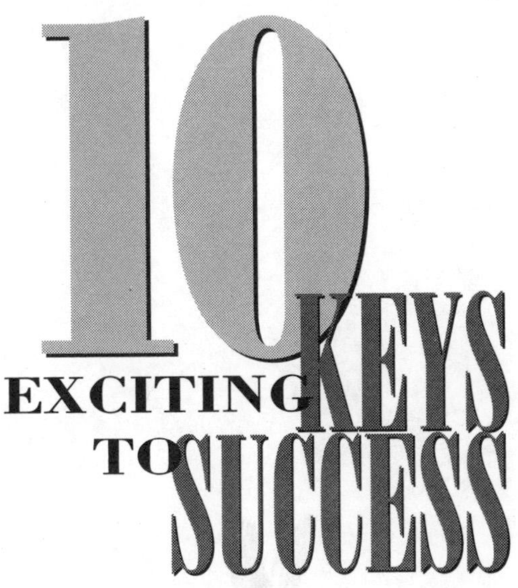

EXCITING KEYS TO SUCCESS

The Power of a Successful Life

BILL NEWMAN

I.S.B.N. 1 875121 13 7

Published by
BILL NEWMAN INTERNATIONAL
P.O. BOX 195
TOOWONG, QLD 4066
Australia
Tel (07) 3371 0750, Fax (07) 3870 1664
International +61 7 3371 0750, +61 7 3870 1664

Dedicated to Ben and Luke
Fly like eagles!

THIS BOOK CAN CHANGE YOUR LIFE!

Often when reading a book we decide to apply what we read to our lives. All too often, weeks later, we have forgotten our good intentions. Here are 5 practical ways of:-

TURNING GOOD INTENTIONS INTO PRACTICAL HABITS

1. USE CARDS

Write out the principles or passages you want to memorise on 3" x 5" cards and review them often.

2. MARK YOUR CALENDAR

Mark your calendar daily for the time when you will review your good intentions.

3. RE-READ YOUR UNDERLINES

Underline key portions of this book, then re-read your underlines over and over.

4. APPLY THE MATERIAL IMMEDIATELY

There is an old saying:

> Hear something - you forget it,
> See something - you remember it, and
> Do something - you understand it.

Apply what you learn as soon as you possibly can - it helps you understand and remember it.

5. PRIORITISE WHAT YOU WANT TO LEARN

Select 1-3 things from the book, apply them faithfully and make them a habit. Remember, every person alive struggles with turning their good intentions into habits. Using these 5 points will turn wishing into doing.

Contents

Preface

No one wants to climb the ladder of success only to discover that theirladder was leaning against the wrong wall!

Success is a series of right choices. Each day we stand at a fork in the road. When we say yes to one activity, we must say no to another.

Effective leadership is the willingness to sacrifice for the sake of predetermined objectives. We must know what we want to achieve and then go for it with single-minded determination.

Elton Trueblood, the great Quaker of yesteryear stated perceptively that:

"Man can bear great physical or spiritual hardship but what he cannot bear is the sense of meaninglessness. We must find some way in which our lives count, in which they seem important, or we will go mad."

Your life can be filled with meaning and purpose. It is my

hope that this book will help you discover what that purpose is. Fill your life with a sense of destiny. Discover what your purpose is. It would be a tragedy to come to the end of your life and realise how much more you could have achieved with your life.

Don't let anybody tell you winning isn't important.

Don't just exist, start to live, and start to win.

Everybody is born with an equal chance to become just as unequal as he or she possibly can be.

In 1936, Jessie Owens came back from the Olympic Games as the world's fastest man. At the huge press conference, the first question asked was, "How did you do it, Jessie? Four gold medals, you embarrassed Hitler in his own hometown, the fastest man in the world...how did you do it?"

"Oh," he said, "I think it all began when I was a kid back in junior high school. My coach got us together and made a speech I've never forgotten. The main thing he said was, 'You can pretty well become whatever you make up your mind to be.' As a junior high kid, I looked up at my coach and shouted, 'Coach, I've already decided what I want to be! The fastest man in the world!' And my coach looked down at me, a skinny, scrawny black boy and said, 'Jessie, that's a great dream. Fact is Jessie, I don't know if I've ever heard such a great dream as that. There's only one problem with your dream, Jessie.'

'What's that, coach?'
'Dreams have a way of floating high in the sky. they just float up there like clouds. Dreams never become realities unless you have the courage to build a ladder to them'
'How do you build a ladder to a dream, coach?'
'Well Jessie,' he said, 'you build it one step a a time'."

By nature, I am a practical person. If it doesn't work, I'm not interested. In this book, there are ten steps that I know really work. They are tried and proven in many lives and are just waiting to be proven in yours.

Let's start right now. These ideas are, to say the least exciting. Don't try to skip any. Take each step as it comes. they will take you all the way to the top. Together let's discover - "The Power of a Successful Life".

Bill Newman

Bill Newman

10 EXCITING KEYS TO SUCCESS

1.` *CONTROL YOUR THOUGHT LIFE*
People become what they think about.

2. *HAVE PRECISE GOALS*
Are you kicking at goals or just keeping score?

3. *CONTROL YOUR SPEECH*
Words condition your thinking and others.
Talk positively

4. *ASSUME RESPONSIBILITY*
Do it now!

5. *OVERCOME PROBLEMS & HURTS*

Don't nurse your hurts
Don't rehearse your hurts
Don't curse your hurts
BUT
Reverse your hurts
Hurts will make you bitter or better

6. *BEFRIEND GOOD MEN*
You grow like the company you keep.

7. *WORK SMARTER - NOT HARDER*
Think. How can I do it better?
The key to success is attention to detail.

8. *DO MORE THAN EXPECTED*
Go the second mile.
The difference between good and great is a little extra effort

9. *KEEP AT IT*
Always too soon to quit.Never give up.Persist.

10. *BE COMMITTED*

Key 1

Control Your Thought Life

PEOPLE BECOME
WHAT THEY THINK ABOUT

Key 1

Control Your Thought Life

I remember once being in the beautiful Victorian city of Bendigo and driving past a circus. Over to the side I saw the huge circus elephants. There was a large elephant tied by a chain to a small stake in the ground. I thought to myself, 'Why, he could easily rip that stake from the earth and be free. Why doesn't he do it?' Then the answer dawned on me. As a small elephant, he could never break free. After much time and pain, his mind was conditioned, he would always be enslaved.

The tragedy is that so many people are like this. They are beaten from the start thinking that they will never amount to much in life. They will never gain skills or accomplishments. They will always have to stay in the same old rut. It's not what we think we are, but what we think we are not, that is often the problem.

Your brain would have to be the most complex mechanism in the world. It is certainly the most influential organ of your body. With it you think, remember, love, hate, feel, reason, imagine and analyse.

The average brain contains about 12 billion cells, each of which is connected to 10,000 other brain cells, totalling 120 trillion brain connections. No wonder a scientist stated, "The human brain is the most complex arrangement of matter in the universe."

Technology, with all its advancement with computers, has not even come close to duplicating its capabilities. The type and content of information you allow to be fed into your brain is tremendously important. The wise writer of Proverbs observed, "As a man thinks in his heart, so is he"

Your brain has three very important functions, your intellect, emotions and will. It is little wonder that with all the negative input into our minds today, we have so much negative reaction to life. I refuse to read the newspaper first thing in the morning because it is filled with bad news. The only success is in the sport pages and even then so many have lost. What a way to start the day.

IF YOU DO NOT CONTROL YOUR THOUGHT LIFE,YOU WILL BE A SLAVE OF YOUR SURROUNDINGS

The saying is so true - "Life responds to our attitudes".

The world's greatest area of undeveloped territory lies beneath people's hats. It was the great Benjamin Disraeli who said, "Nurture your mind with great thoughts, for you never go any higher than you think." The choice is ours whether our thoughts will be constructive or destructive and will determine the ultimate result of our lives.

IF YOU WANT TO BE SUCCESSFUL YOU MUST THINK UNTIL IT HURTS

To control your mind, to make time to think, is just plain hard work but the fantastic results cannot be measured. Most of us are mentally lazy by nature. We always choose the path of least resistance. Once you overcome the inertia of getting your mind ticking then the hard grind is over. The thinking apparatus has become trained.

Your mind is like a muscle. It must be exercised to grow. This has been one of the greatest discoveries of my life. Don't limit your potential. As you exercise your body to develop, grow and keep healthy, so learn to stretch your mind. What you don't use, you lose.

One of the greatest ways to develop your mind is through reading. Remember - leaders are readers.

THINK AHEAD OF TIME

Pre-plan your mind to act in situations ahead of time. If you get too much change, you would give it back. If you had the opportunity to read unwholesome literature, you would refuse it. Precondition your mind ahead - it really works.

TAKE TIME TO THINK - IT IS THE SOURCE OF POWER

Don't say you haven't time to spend thinking. Time given to thought is the greatest time saver of all. A woodsman never loses time when he sharpens his axe.

OVERCOME WORRY, DOUBT AND FEAR

The three worst mental enemies you will have to fight and conquer are worry, doubt and fear. You face them every day. They will waste your time and sap your strength.

TODAY IS THE TOMORROW YOU WORRIED ABOUT YESTERDAY

There is an old Swedish proverb that says worry often gives a small thing a big shadow.

Here are the keys to overcoming worry, doubt and fear.

1. Clearly analyse the concern you have.
2. Evaluate the possible outcome.
3. Establish whether they truly have any substance or not.
4. Is it a fear of the past or a fear of the future?

Remember 40% of the things we worry about never happen, 30% are in the past and cannot be helped, 12% concern the affairs of others that aren't our business, 10% are about sickness, real or imagined, and 8% are worth worrying about. Attack the 8% with faith and action and you can eliminate most of the worries, doubts and fears that seek to prevent your happiness and the attainment of your goals.

The mind is the most delicate, the most sensitive instrument in all creation. Just as the body is what the body is fed, in the same way the mind is what the mind is fed.

LEARN TO THINK BIG

Petty minded people never really succeed in life. Even some people I know who are in top positions are really quite small in their thinking. Their quality of life is way down. Keep your mind focused on big objectives. You may win arguments but not friends. You can prove your marriage partner wrong by winning arguments but drive away peace and happiness from your marriage. You may make major issues out of minor errors with a student or employee, but fail to develop their potential.

Big men do not laugh at big ideas. People who tell you it cannot be done are almost always unsuccessful people. They are often strictly average or mediocre at best in terms of accomplishment. Be extra cautious about this.

Don't allow negative thinking people to destroy your plan to think your way to success. They are everywhere and they seem to delight in sabotaging the positive progress of others. Often they feel inadequate in themselves, so they want to make a mediocre person out of you.

"DON'T LET THE DISSENTERS BE THE DECIDERS"

You are judged by the company you keep. Birds of a feather flock together. Be sure you are in the flock that thinks right.

THROW THE THOUGHT POISON OUT OF YOUR ENVIRONMENT

Each of us is responsible for our attitude and mental outlook. The body produces substances called "endorphins" that operate at different sites in the brain and in the spinal cord. They reduce the experience of pain and censor out unpleasant stimuli. In fact the presence of endorphins,which are secreted by the brain, actually causes a feeling of well being. Researchers today have learned that optimistic thoughts and positive attitudes can stimulate the production of endorphins.

Control your thought life, don't let it control you. Picture the person you want to become and move toward becoming that kind of person. If you see yourself a failure - a failure you will be. If you see yourself as someone with purpose and direction in life then that is the kind of person you are becoming.

"AS A MAN THINKS IN HIS HEART - SO IS HE"

Never surrender your dreams to noisy negatives.

Key
2

Have Precise Goals

ARE YOU KICKING AT GOALS
OR JUST KEEPING SCORE?

Key
2

Have Precise Goals

The saying is quite true - if you fail to plan, you plan to fail. Can you imagine what a basketball or football game would be like without goals? Absolute bedlam! Goal setting is one of the most important steps in achieving success. What do you hope to do or be in 20 years, 10 years, 5 years, 2 or 1 year from now, or even 6 months? Set monthly, daily, even hourly goals. It becomes exciting to see so many of the things you desire realised.

Some time ago my son Ben was laboriously going over his times tables. I said, "Ben, the only way to master maths is to master your times tables". I asked him to set his watch for twenty minutes, give his total attention and effort for that time and then he was free to go and play. Twenty minutes later he had mastered the difficult tables and was out happily playing. What happened? He set a goal in a specific time frame and achieved results. That is all that goal setting is.

ARE YOU KICKING AT GOALS OR JUST KEEPING SCORE

Here are some suggestions to get you started in the exciting discovery and potential of goal setting. Make a list of the goals in your life. Dream some dreams. Here are a few ideas.

- To become a better parent, husband or wife.
- To better my job situation.
- To obtain a better education.
- To increase my reading schedule this year.
- To be an excellent teacher, doctor, etc.
- To become the best mechanic in the shop.
- To get the job I want.
- To play the piano.
- To obtain my own business, etc etc.

Now rearrange them in order of priority, the goals you want first. Then set a target date. Be realistic. Make them attainable goals. (For example, you cannot join the Police Force if you do not have the required height!!)

GOAL	DATE
1	
2	
3	
4	
5	
6	
7	
8	
9	
10	
11	
12	
13	
14	
15	

Now that you have listed your goals, take a separate piece of clean paper (one for each goal) and write your goal at the top of the page. Next, write the following headings with even spacing down the page (see below):

GOAL No 1

ACTIONS

1

2

3

4

Qualities I need to obtain my Goal

1

2

3

4

Deficiencies to Conquer

1

2

3

4

Action Required

Now make a list of the required action you must take to achieve your goal.

Remember, no gain without pain. For example, the extra effort required to achieve your goal, more education, to save systematically the cash required for a course, etc.

Qualities I Will Need to Achieve my Goal

The next step - Write down and develop the qualities in your personal behaviour that will be required to achieve your goal. Visualise the new you. For example, a pleasant personality, neat appearance, mental awareness, hard work, etc.

Present Deficiencies to Conquer

Now that you have your goal clearly defined and know what must be done to achieve this goal, identify some present deficiencies that you are aware of. Don't be too hard on yourself, but honestly evaluate the obstacles that might prevent you from achieving these goals. Now you can go to work on your goals and when these things pop up, you will have an action plan to conquer them. For example, laziness, time wasting, critical tongue, impatience, etc.

Do the same for each goal that you have identified on the previous page. Keep your sheets of paper handy in your diary or somewhere close by so you can look and see the progress you are making.

Develop an inner will to follow through your plans regardless of obstacles, criticism or circumstances. Do not worry about what other people say, think or do. You must develop a burning desire for the things you want in life.

In the absence of clearly defined goals, we are forced to concentrate on activity and ultimately become enslaved by it. Remember, there is no joy in victory without running the risk of defeat.

OPPORTUNITIES NEVER COME TO THOSE WHO WAIT. THEY ARE CAPTURED BY THOSE WHO DARE TO ATTACK.

The fulfilment of our goals must be good for others. If they bring harm to others, then our goals are selfish. The great rewards in life are love and achievement. All else is secondary. Become a giver - not a getter.

DON'T BE AFRAID TO SET GOALS

To achieve goals demands hard work, determination and commitment. For many, though, the main reason they do not establish a quest to achieve goals is plain fear, the fear of ridicule from others or the fear of defeat. Others fear their goals will not be perfect - or worse still they may consider themselves presumptuous.

Establish **S-M-A-R-T** goals.
Make your goals:-

Specific
Measurable
Attainable
Realistic
Tangible

You can't manage what you can't measure. When performance is measured, performance improves. A leader and a winner is someone who turns resources into results.

The importance and the benefits of goal setting are immeasurable. Without setting goals your visions and dreams are just wishful thinking. The main benefits of goal setting are that they make decision-making easier. Your physical health is better because you have established a positive attitude to life. Your mental health is so much better. You eliminate stress, confusion and fear. Those who have goals attract respect from people. It gives you a sense of accomplishment; it gives you "stickability' and staying power. It is staying power that sets leaders apart.

STAY MOTIVATED

Your degree of motivation is only as high as your opinion of your goals. A lack of passionate belief in your goals can quench your desire to succeed and paralyse your progress.

The tragedy of life doesn't lie in not reaching your goal; the tragedy lies in having no goal to reach.

START NOW!!

HENRY KAISER SAID "DETERMINE WHAT YOU WANT MORE THAN ANYTHING ELSE IN LIFE, WRITE DOWN THE MEANS BY WHICH YOU INTEND TO ATTAIN IT, AND PERMIT NOTHING TO DETER YOU FROM PURSUING IT."

Key 3

CONTROL YOUR SPEECH

WORDS CONDITION YOUR THINKING AND OTHERS: SO TALK POSITIVELY

Key 3

Control Your Speech

One of the most amazing facts of life is that our speech determines our direction in life. Not only does it determine our thinking but it influences so many others that we contact day by day.

I remember once speaking to a group of men in prison. I said, "Most of you men are here because your parents, relatives, or so-called friends said that you would end up in gaol". They looked at me in disbelief thinking I had a crystal ball. One man said, "My parents said one day I would end up in prison and I didn't want to disappoint them!!" I would estimate conservatively that 90% of prisoners have had that experience.

THE TONGUE CONTROLS YOUR LIFE.

We can say, "I hate you!" or "I love you!"

These are only words but they are powerful words. Which ones do you like spoken to you? What effects do they have on you?

Remember - what you say is what you get. To control your mouth you must first control your mind. Right or wrong thinking is the basis for controlling your words.

Whatever we sow we reap. If we criticise people we will reap criticism. If we are judgemental with people we will be judged. If we encourage people we , in turn, will be encouraged. If we show care, love and concern we, in turn, will enjoy the fruits.

The computer of our mind needs to be constantly reprogrammed with positive input.

Words are the most powerful things in the universe.

The words we speak will either hold us in bondage or bring us into success. Examine your vocabulary.

The following statements have been used by so many to stop them attaining their true potential in life:

* I am not smart enough for that.
* I cannot do anything about my temper.
* I will never be able to have that.
* I could not possibly do that, etc., etc.

You see - words are either creative or destructive. Words, and the way you speak, can make a real difference in your life.

> As you think, so do you speak. As you speak, so do you act. As you act, so goes your future.

The words you speak about yourself and your circumstances can literally change things. They can make the difference between defeat and success.

Speech filled with fear, doubt, unbelief and negativism can cause defeat in your life.

On the other hand words filled with optimism, hope and belief will shape a positive future for you.

Words determine your attitude.

Spoken words "programme" your heart for either success or defeat. Little by little you CAN change things in your life which will change your future. Positive words are like the rudder on a ship. They can turn it in another direction.

While words are no substitute for hard work and perseverance they will, however, determine your attitude and, remember, your attitude confirms your ***vision.***

"If you keep on saying things are going to be hard you have a good chance of being a prophet." - Isaac Singer

The input that we place in others people's minds is so powerful. There was a milkman in the U.S.A. who would run up to a certain house and as he delivered the milk, would ruffle the curly hair of a little girl saying, "How's my little Miss America this morning?" He said it so constantly, that the girl went on to become Miss America!

Married couples can destroy each other by public put downs and cutting words. For example, "It's great that you have come for lunch today - at least we get a good meal!!" etc. etc.

Parents can annihilate the self esteem of their children. "Look at Johnny, can't even tie up his laces yet." Johnny is saying to himself, "Yes I'm hopeless, I'm hopeless."

Teachers can belittle the students. Bosses can destroy relationships with employees with continual criticism and little praise.

THE IMPORTANCE OF PRAISE FROM PARENTS

The key elements of self-esteem are belonging, worth and confidence. Belonging comes from our relationship at home; worth comes from what we are intrinsically, confidence comes from what we can do - our achievements.

Children must be constantly affirmed.

You praise children for what they do, for the efforts they make to improve in their abilities.

Can you praise too much? Absolutely not. Not if the praise is legitimate and sincere. It must not be flattery or manipulation.

Studies have shown that for every negative thing you say to a child, you must say four positive things to keep the balance.

Parents, don't nitpick and don't criticise.

ALL OF US HAVE FORMULATED A MENTAL IMAGE OF OURSELVES BASED ON THE FEELINGS OF ACCEPTANCE WE RECEIVE FROM OUR PARENTS.

TEENAGERS CAN DESTROY EACH OTHER

The ages of thirteen to fourteen years can be the most disastrous in a person's life. It is at this time that young teenagers turn on each other and become so critical. They leave primary school and go into high school with hopes and ambitions. Pity help the struggling teen at this point. "Is that a banana on your face or a nose?" etc. etc. This is the age when parents, teachers and friends of young teenagers have to work particularly hard with encouragement and help.

YOUR TOTAL UNIQUENESS

You are so special

Have you ever considered just how special you are even in your physical body?
For instance:-

YOUR EARS:

Your ears are still growing, even though the other parts of your body have stopped. If you lived to be 1,000 years your ears would be as large as an elephant.

YOUR HAIR:

The hair on your head is as strong as aluminium. A narrow stretch of rope woven from human hair has supported the weight of a small car.

YOUR SKULL:

Your skull is as strong as steel though proportionately it weighs only one fifth as much.

YOUR EYES:

You think you've got nice, big, blue eyes: Not so, blue eyes are really red and only appear to be blue. The iris, the coloured part of the eye, is covered with tiny blood vessels which, seen through the cornea at the front of the eye, look blue.

YOUR TEETH:

The hardest part of your body is the enamel on your teeth; it is even harder than ivory.

YOUR HANDS:

Your hands are probably your most complex instruments, capable of performing thousands of jobs with precision. Just to grasp something brings into play a host of muscles, joints and tendons - from the shoulders to the fingertips. Taking a spoonful of soup, for instance, involves more than 30 joints and 50 muscles.

YOUR FEET:

During an average day, your feet take a sledgehammer pounding equivalent to more than 1,000 tonnes. They can support the weight of a 90kg man on a base less than 310 square centimetres without fatigue. This is achieved by an astonishing arrangement of bones and joints - for a quarter of all your bones in your body are in your feet.

YOUR HEART:

The human heart beats about 100,000 times a day and about 40 million times a year. Normally it beats 70 times to the minute, but it often changes its rate to keep pace with music or the rapid beat of drums. It can be made to pulse to almost any rhythm and automatically picks up the beat.

You may not have noticed it, but you are a little lop-sided. Usually the left leg is a shade shorter than the right. One arm is longer, one ear bigger and there is likely to be more hair on one side of the head than the other.

NO-ONE EVEN SMELLS LIKE YOU!

That's how your dog knows who you are! Let's face it - you are special.

TALK POSITIVELY

Not only is it important to talk positively to others but it is essential to talk positively to yourself and to express yourself in a positive way. A woman, as she was sitting down, placed a cup of coffee on the floor beside her saying the words - "Now watch me spill that." You can be sure that she spilt it!

A wise employer would never employ a person with a dirty mouth. They know that if that person could not control his/her tongue then you could not trust him/her in controlling their sticky fingers on the job.

An employer can not afford the luxury of a negative speaking critical employee on staff. In no time flat many in the organisation are thinking negatively and not positively.

I love the reply of those who, when asked to do something, say - "No problem." Learn to use affirmative speech. It will transform your life and others. Forget the words 'I cannot' but use instead 'I can' and 'I will'.

We have all seen leading sports people on television in an interview professing the fact that they are going to win. Verbal affirmation makes all the difference.

STAY ON THE POSITIVE SIDE WHEN YOU TALK ABOUT PEOPLE

If you haven't got a good thing to say about a person, then don't say anything. To be successful, you must eliminate gossip from your vocabulary. You can test if you are prone to be a gossip by taking this test:

1. Do I spread rumours about other people?

2. Do I always have good things to say about others?

3. Do I like to hear reports of a scandal?

4. Do I judge others only on the basis of facts?

5. Do I encourage others to bring their rumours to me?

6. Do I precede conversations with "don't tell anybody?"

7. Do I keep confidential information confidential?

8. Do I feel guilty about what I say concerning others?

Taking an axe and chopping up your neighbours' furniture will not make your furniture look one bit better.

Start today by determining to talk positively. Don't be discouraged if you slip once in a while! Work on it for thirty days and see the dramatic difference it makes in your life by talking positively.

Self control is an essential attitude and characteristic for a leader. The control of the tongue is paramount.

I have a dear friend who always thrills me when I ask him how he is going. His reply is, "I feel terrific, but tomorrow I am going to be even better".

Action often precedes the feeling. Talk positively and watch your attitude change. Your day goes the way the corners of your mouth turn. A healthy attitude is contagious - don't wait to catch it from others - be a carrier!

WHAT YOU SAY IS WHAT YOU ARE

Key 4

Assume Responsibility

DO IT NOW

Key
4

ASSUME RESPONSIBILITY

Assuming responsibility is one the great keys to success. The easiest course of action is to allow others to take the lead. Remember:-

THERE IS NO GAIN WITHOUT PAIN

So determine *now* to be a responsible person.

Since time began, we have pushed responsibility on to others. Growth and development comes only by discipline and responsibility. The best helping hand you can find is at the end of your own arm.

**LOSERS LET IT HAPPEN -
WINNERS MAKE IT HAPPEN**

What are some of the attitudes of a responsible person?

1. *Be Appreciative*

Develop a gratitude attitude. I wish all young people could start work with "McDonalds" for 6 months to learn how to say please and thank you. Do not take people and their service to you for granted. Say thank you to people. Write notes. Take time to call or phone someone who has given you a kindness.

2. *Be Kind*

Don't cut, don't criticise. "Do unto others as you would have them do unto you" is the Master's advice and it cannot be beaten.

IT TAKES LITTLE SIZE TO CRITICISE

On an office door were written the words - 'Come in without knocking, go out the same way'!! Remember, if you throw mud you lose ground. Teenagers destroy each other by their sarcastic and cutting words. Rudeness is a weak man's imitation of strength.

3. *Be Complimentary*

Be on the lookout all the time for something to praise someone for. 'That dress colour really suits you'. 'My, your house is so lovely'. 'You did a great job with that assignment'. Don't fake it, make it sincere. Mean it and watch people grow. The reward you receive will be so worthwhile.

4. *Be Genuinely Interested in Others*

People with discernment can always tell whether you are tuned in when talking to them even on the phone. I know if someone on the other end of the phone is writing or involved with something else while talking to me. When talking with someone, even if it is in a crowded room (that's where often we have our best conversations), concentrate on that one person. If necessary, ask that you don't be disturbed. Take the phone off the hook. Be there - not elsewhere in your mind and people will love and respect you for it.

DEVELOP AN ABOVE AVERAGE HANDSHAKE

When someone shakes your hand, don't let it feel like a dead fish. Take it firmly and use eye contact.

Remember people's names. This really requires effort.

THE SWEETEST WORD IN THE ENGLISH LANGUAGE IS A PERSON'S NAME

A person who can remember faces and names is streets ahead of others. Be determined to develop a good memory. Here's how:-

a) You have to be interested. If it is important, you will remember it. If it is the name of your new boss, you will remember it!

b) Concentrate. Focus your thoughts.

c) Repetition. Say it over and over. Write it down if necessary.

d) Association. Attach the name to mental pictures. If someone for example has the name Walker, picture in your mind someone walking.

e) Remembering a person's name is so important. Some of us have to work at it harder than others.

5. *Be Ethical*

Have integrity. Shakespeare said, "To thine own self be true". Your good character is one of your greatest assets. Keep your word.

Those who are given to white lies soon become colour blind.

THE TRUE TEST OF A PERSON'S CHARACTER IS WHAT THEY ARE LIKE WHEN THEY ARE ALONE

Always tell the truth and you never have to remember what you said.

6. *Be Friendly*

"If a man would have friends he must show himself friendly". Risk making the first move.

**WITHOUT REAL FRIENDS,
EVEN A MILLIONAIRE IS POOR**

Life is an experience in relationships. The big problem often is a lack of self worth in many, making it hard to reach out kindly to others. Don't wait for others to come to you. You can't buy friends but real friendship takes time and effort and is so worthwhile.

7. *Be Enthusiastic*

The power of enthusiasm is fantastic. Like grease on the axle of a wheel. It smoothes your journey to your goals. People will respond to your excitement.

Constantly feed your enthusiam with books, tapes and association with motivated enthusiastic peolple.

Remember - attitudes are contagious. Let yourself get excited.

Without enthusiasm life would be dull like lemonade without the fizz. The enthusiasm of my children's approach to life thrills me so much. Enthusiasm requires daring. The world belongs to the person who is enthusiastic about life.

Negative attitudes are absolutely poisonous to the body, they can actually lead to physical illnesses and emotional breakdowns.

I firmly believe in order to develop an attitude that will turn your life around, one of the most important ingredients is enthusiasm. Persistence, ability, brains, etc. are important but without enthusiasm even the greatest ideas can become bogged down.

Enthusiasm changes problems to challenges.
Enthusiasm creates enthusiasm in others.
Enthusiasm rids the mind of worry and tension.
Enthusiasm improves your
outlook on life.
Enthusiasm forgets yesterday
and attacks today.

SO -

THINK ENTHUSIASTICALLY

8. Be Natural

If you are tense, the vibes radiate out to others. As you relax, others relax also. Throw away the mask and be yourself.

BE YOURSELF
BUT BE YOUR BEST SELF

Don't pretend to be what you are not. People sense it and don't appreciate it.

9. *Be Happy - Smile*

When you shake hands take the hand firmly - look the person in the eye and smile. A smile says, "I'm O.K., you're O.K." Your smile is one of your greatest natural assets. Use it. Economically it takes less muscles to smile and more to frown. I see happier faces on poison bottles than on people at times! Practise smiling and see the difference it makes in your day - and others. Don't look like you have just visited your bank manager or your shoes are too tight. So many look like they have been baptised in lemon juice.

10. *Be Well Groomed*

Make your appearance an asset - not a liability. Do you buy the torn, top newspaper on the pile or the one further down? Do you select a nice apple in the shop or a pitted one? People want the best. Your appearance communicates.

YOU HAVE ONLY ONE CHANCE AT A GOOD FIRST IMPRESSION

It is to your advantage to make a good first impression. If you are well dressed, it adds to your self confidence. How do we know what to wear? The key is appropriateness. You wouldn't wear what you would wear to the beach to a business meeting. Read up on dress in a good book. It will save you a lot of money. Shop around. They needn't cost the earth but make sure your clothes are clean and pressed. Keep your shoes clean polished and in good repair. Good grooming starts from the shoes up. Keep your nails clean and neatly trimmed. Keep your glasses clean (if you wear them).

I know it is a free world and you can wear and look how you like, but like it or not, man looks on the outward appearance. Make your appearance work for you. Hair, regardless of style, should be clean and washed. When you look good, you feel good and you act good.

11. *Be Rational - Balanced*

The beauty of a balanced life is a great quality to have. Keep your temper to yourself, no one else wants it. Don't keep darting off into every direction. The apostle Paul said, "this one thing I do."

THIS ONE THING I DO
NOT THOSE HUNDRED THINGS
I DABBLE AT

Take time to be quiet, to weigh up things. People will not have confidence in you if you are impetuous.

12. *Be Time Conscious - Be Punctual*

To be turning up late constantly reveals a selfish person or an undisciplined or unorganised individual. If you are one minute late to a meeting where 100 people are gathered, you have wasted 100 minutes. The amount of time lost at meetings and church services is unbelievable. Respect the time of others. This is my most precious earthly gift. If I give you my time, I am giving you something money cannot fully buy. It may be helpful to establish a time table.

WHAT YOU DON'T USE - YOU LOSE

Don't waste time. Use it. It is precious.

13. *Be Prepared*

Abraham Lincoln once said 'I will prepare myself and one day my chance will come'. The boy scouts taught me to 'be prepared'. Have in your mind, before you meet people, what you will ask or say. If you are travelling into the city, have parking meter cash. Think ahead. Condition your mind before an event then you will make the right decision under pressure. Pity the person who has not stored up ahead of time the resources he or she will need when crisis comes, spiritually, financially and in every other way.

14. *Be Need Conscious*

Selfishness is one of the greatest problems in society today. We live in a country where there are needs all around. Don't live with the idea "What can I get out of this?"

**NOT WHAT CAN I GET
BUT WHAT CAN I GIVE**

There are two types of people in life - the givers and the takers. Become a giver and the world will love you. Read history. The ones who contributed to society are the ones remembered fondly.

So become a responsible person. As Zig Zigler says 'Become a meaningful specific - not a wandering generality'.

**THE MOST IMPORTANT LETTER
IN THE ALPHABET IS THE LETTER "W".
IT CHANGES A "NO" TO A "NOW"**

So -

“DO IT NOW”

Key
5

Overcome Problems and Hurts

DON'T NURSE YOUR HURTS
DON'T REHEARSE YOUR HURTS
DON'T CURSE YOUR HURTS
BUT
REVERSE YOUR HURTS
BECAUSE
HURTS WILL MAKE YOU
BITTER OR BETTER

Key
5

Overcome Problems and Hurts

The only place in town where people do not have any problems is out at the local cemetery. Problems are part of life. The key is to turn problems into opportunities, lemons into lemonade.

You and I know of many who, despite overwhelming problems with their health, mental abilities, background or education, have made a tremendous impact in this world.

Every problem has within it the seed of its own solution. A successful man will never see the day that does not bring a fresh quota of problems. The mark of success is to deal with them effectively.

Some men work hard and save money so their sons will not have the problems that made great men of their fathers. Accept problems as a challenge.

HOW TO SOLVE PROBLEMS

Use these six steps:

1. *Don't Fear The Problem.*
   Calm down. Negative thinking is no way to solve a problem. A cool calm mind thinks better than a worried mind.

2. *Study and Analyse The Problem.*
   Get advice. Get the right facts. Get the issues clear. Don't allow your mind to be cluttered.

3. *Concentrate On The Solution.*
   Far too many people over dwell on the problem and give no thought to a solution. Don't blame yourself or others or circumstances. Many of the biggest problems are cured by simple solutions.

4. *Proceed From The Known To The Unknown.*
   Use your knowledge of how you solved previous problems to help you with this one.

5. *Select A Solution That Is Good For Others As Well As For Yourself.*
   It will build better relationships and benefit all concerned.

6. *Act.*
   The sooner you act, the sooner the problem will be solved. Act, even if a little risk is necessary.

You may have personal or business problems which may be getting you down. Take some time out to go to a hospital or a friend who has greater problems. You will come back feeling that your problems aren't all that great.

Problem solving can be fun. It adds spice to life which might otherwise be boredom. Don't be part of the problem. Be the solution.

TURN THE PROBLEM INTO A PROPELLER

OVERCOME YOUR HURTS

There would not be a single person that has lived on this earth who has not been hurt. Perhaps your marriage has broken up. Your parents have separated. Someone you love has belittled you or you endure constant criticism.

Remember - when you are getting kicked from the rear it means you are in front. Pay no attention to what the critics say, no statue has ever been erected to a critic. If you think about it, there are just two days in which the average person is free from criticism - the day he is born and the day he dies.

HOW TO HANDLE AND LEARN FROM CRITICISM

1. What were they actually criticising?

2. Were there facts to back up the statements?

3. Was it logical?

4. Were the examples one-sided?

5. Did they lump facts and opinions together?

6. Did they over-generalise?

7. Were their conclusions valid?

8. Was the criticism over-negative in character or did they make positive suggestions that you might be able to implement?

9. Will your performance be improved by following the advice given?

IF YOU ARE IN THE FRONT LINE YOU ARE THE FIRST TO GET SHOT AT

We can have many compliment us for something, yet it only needs one person to criticise us and we forget all the encouragement and think only on the cutting remark. We cannot afford the luxury.

DON'T NURSE YOUR HURTS
Throw them away and replace them with positive attitudes. Self pity will destroy you and others whom you live with.

DON'T REHEARSE YOUR HURTS
Going over and over your problems only turns them from a molehill to a mountain.

DON'T CURSE YOUR HURTS
You can't help the past but you can change the future.

REVERSE YOUR HURTS
You may have come from behind but you can pass the group and go to the lead.

Remember:

HURTS WILL MAKE YOU BITTER OR BETTER

Learn to forgive others. Jesus Christ was the supreme example. Why even on the cross, He cried out "Father, forgive them, they don't know what they are doing."

EXPERIENCING FORGIVENESS IS ONE OF THE GREATEST NEEDS IN THE WORLD TODAY

Take another step - If you have hurt someone, be big enough to go and apologise. Ask forgiveness, say, "I'm sorry."

It has been well said that the three hardest tasks in the world are neither physical feats nor intellectual achievements, but moral acts: To return love for hate, to include the excluded, and to say, "I was wrong."

Key 6

BEFRIEND GOOD MEN

YOU GO LIKE THE COMPANY YOU KEEP

Key
6

Befriend Good Men

I had the privilege of attending a National breakfast in Washington D.C. While I was there, I drove past the famous Watergate buildings and my mind went back to those tragic days during the Nixon administration. He lost the Presidency because he listened to the advice and counsel of untrustworthy men.

There is no truer saying than - "you go like the company you keep", so choose good friends. If you run with the wrong crowd, young person, they may pull you down before you pull them up. Choose carefully your friends.

Peer pressure is not only a great problem amongst our young people, we all are affected by it. The office party or the pressure to succeed, can cause you to drop standards and to compromise.

Look carefully at the closest associations in your life, for that is the direction you are heading.

Success in life depends upon the support and help of other people. No one makes it alone.

IF YOU WANT FRIENDS IN LIFE YOU MUST SHOW YOURSELF TO BE FRIENDLY

WORK HARD AT BUILDING SUCCESSFUL RELATIONSHIPS

Without friendship one is doomed to loneliness. Value your friendships. Tell your friends you appreciate them. A friend is like an island of safety where you feel secure and where communicating is often without sound.

FRIENDSHIP IS THE INEXPRESSIBLE COMFORT OF FEELING SAFE WITH A PERSON, HAVING NEITHER TO WEIGH THOUGHTS NOR MEASURE WORDS
George Elliott

Work on relationships constantly. Don't take a friend for granted. Unless it is kept constantly polished up then a relationship can get a little dusty or rusted. Use the phone, a letter or a visit, card or gift. Work hard with the relationships in your marriage, family, with your parents or with your children. Those in your work situation may need a little extra care.

A successful relationship is based on mutual respect. Recognise your own self-worth and the self-worth of others.

A friend is one who puts his finger on a fault without rubbing it in. There is an old Chinese proverb - "Do not use a hatchet to remove a fly from your friend's forehead."

MY BEST FRIEND IS THE ONE WHO BRINGS OUT THE BEST IN ME
Henry Ford

To gain friends, become interested in other people instead of trying to get them interested in you. Friendship is not only doing something for someone, but it is caring for someone, which is what every person needs.

One of the great problems we face today in modern society is the scarcity of good friends. It takes a lot of forgiving to be a friend. Friendship is the art of overlooking the failings of others.

HOW TO MAKE FRIENDS

1. Be likable. Practise being the kind of person people like.

2. Take the initiative. Risk making the first move. Introduce yourself at every opportunity.

3. Get the others person's name straight and make sure they get your name straight.

4. Don't expect anyone to be perfect. Accept human differences and limitations.

5. Find qualities to admire in a person.

6. Practise conversation. Encourage others to talk.

7. Practise being courteous all the time.

A blessed thing it is for any man or woman to have a friend: one human soul whom we can trust utterly; who knows the best and the worst of us, and who loves us in spite of all our faults; who will speak the honest truth to us, while the world flatters us to our face, and laughs at us behind our back; who will give us counsel and reproof in the day of prosperity and self-conceit; but who will cheer us in the day of difficulty and sorrow, when the world leaves us alone to fight our own battle as we can.

- Charles Kingsley

HOW TO BUILD A FRIENDSHIP

Here are a few basic principles to be used in forging friendships.

1. *Develop An Attitude Of Acceptance.*

Accept your friends as they are - warts and all. During the Korean war, the phone rang one day in a fashionable home on the east coast of the United States. To her astonished delight, the woman answering found herself speaking to her son. There had been long months of silence during his absence in Korea, and now she was both startled and delighted to hear that he was in San Diego, on his way home.

"Mom, I just wanted to let you know that I'm bringing a buddy home with me. He got hurt pretty bad, and he has only one eye, one arm and one leg. I'd sure like him to live with us."

"Sure, son," she replied. "He sounds like a brave man. We can find room for him for a while."

"Mom, you don't understand. I want him to come live with us."

"Well, O.K.," she relented. "We could try it for six months or so."

"No, Mom. I want him to stay always. He needs us. He's only got one arm, one leg, and one eye. He's really in bad shape." His mother lost patience. "Son, you're being pretty unrealistic about this. You're being emotional because you've been in the war. That boy will be a drag on you and a problem for all of us. Be reasonable."

Suddenly the phone clicked dead. The next day the parents received from the Navy a telegram that crushed them. The night before, their son had leaped to his death from the twelfth floor of a San Diego hotel. A week later they received the body and looked down with unspeakable sorrow on the corpse of their one-eyed, one-armed, one-legged son.

('Quality Friendship' - Gary Inrig, P.52, Moody Press)

Conditional acceptance destroys people. Remember God accepts us unconditionally on the basis of the finished work of the Lord Jesus.

2. Develop Mutual Attraction.

There are certain people with whom you will feel you click.

3. Develop commitment.

It seems to me that women in our society are more skilled in forming deep relationships than men are. However many men need the security and support that comes from a solid friendship. If you want a deep and lasting friendship, show commitment.

4. Develop Genuine Openness

I know there will be a risk but the rewards are great. When I open my life to someone else, I am giving myself away and that is costly. But how much more costly is it not to give? Throw away the masks.

5. Develop Appreciation and Enjoyment.

Delight in the success of your friends.

HOW NOT TO CHOOSE A FRIEND

There is a danger that we will open our lives to the wrong kind of people. It simply is not true that we need all the friends we can get.

1. Learn To Stand Alone.

Those who are best equipped for friendship are those most prepared to stand alone. A person should be committed to stand firm for his convictions, whatever the cost in terms of popularity or social acceptance.

2. Learn To Say NO.

People are not morally neutral. They either influence our lives for good or for evil.

3. Learn Who To Stay Away From.

a) The Gossip

Avoid the gossip. If they are not loyal to others, they will not be loyal to you.

b) The Quick-Tempered

The wise writer of the Proverbs said:
"Do not associate with a man given to anger, or go with a hot-tempered man, lest you learn his way, and find a name for yourself."

c) The Disloyal
Loyalty is one of the greatest virtues in a friendship. Give it and expect it.

d) The Discontented
Watch the whiner, the complainer, those who constantly maintain a bad attitude to authority or circumstances.

5. The Self-Indulgent
Keep away from selfish people who are wrapped up in themselves, their wants and wishes.

6. The Immoral
With friends like this, you are on the way to disaster. If they want you to read that dirty book, see the dirty film or listen to the dirty language, you cannot help being affected for the worst.

LOOK CAREFULLY AT THE CLOSEST ASSOCIATIONS IN YOUR LIFE - FOR THAT IS THE WAY YOU ARE HEADING

THE OTHER SIDE

Your friends will stretch your vision or choke your dreams. - "The companion of fools will suffer harm. He who walks with wise men will be wise."

The choice is yours.

Key 7

Work Smarter Not Harder

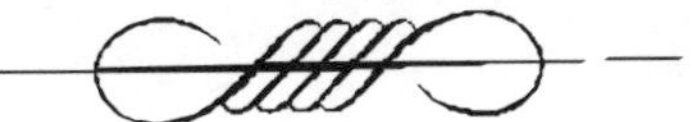

THE KEY TO SUCCESS IS ATTENTION TO DETAIL

Key
7

WORK SMARTER -NOT HARDER

Why is it that we find it hard to get out of bed in the morning to go to work, school or college, yet if we are going fishing we can get up without any problem at 5a.m.? The difference of course is motivation. We do what we really want to do. The secret to life is to apply enthusiasm and energy into every area of our daily life. If we have to be in the office, shop or class for eight hours or more each day, let's enjoy it. Attack, rather than let the situation defeat us.

The self-motivated person determines the direction to go and their action to achieve it. I often say to the young people in high school:-

THIS WORLD DOES NOT OWE YOU A LIVING YOU HAVE TO GET OUT THERE AND MAKE A LIVING

Oftentimes we have to work harder and smarter, at least in the beginning. Develop the attitude that work is fun and enjoyable - which it is. I will always be grateful to my dear father who taught, by example, the work ethic to me. "Son," he would often say, "hard work has never hurt anyone" and he was right. Tension, frustration and pressure can be brought under control but plain hard work is good for your physical and mental health.

THE ONLY PLACE WHERE SUCCESS COMES BEFORE WORK IS IN THE DICTIONARY

It seems the harder you work, the luckier you get.
The general attitude is to get as much as possible for as little effort as possible. It just does not work that way.

However, don't spend a dollar's worth of time for ten cents worth of resultts.

WORK SMARTER

Where would the world be today without the application and thought to solid work effort and learning how to do it better? We would still be riding horses instead of driving cars. (Maybe that would be a good thing!) Think of the tremendous leaps ahead in technology and medical science to name a few. In everything you apply yourself to, ask the question, "How can I do it better?" The biggest hindrance to advancement is the old answer, "But we have always done it this way".

MOTIVATING YOURSELF INTO ACTION

The motivated person must have that personal quality of initiative, that drive that pushes him from a position of inertia to action.

1. Become a Self-Starter

If you go to the museums, you will see the old cars and trucks that they had to crank to get started. Then they developed the automatic ignition. The question is, are you a self-starter, or do you wait around for someone to crank your engine? Learn to be a self-starter. When you get up in the morning, seize the day before it seizes you.

2. Give it all you have got.

Far too often we expend half the energy we should - we do things half-heartedly. Remember, if you are competing with another person, company or business, you not only have to give it all you have, but you have to give it even more than the other person.

Make ***devotion, determination and dedication*** a way of life for you. Mix with the whole thing a good helping of enthusiasm and you have the recipe for success for you in life.

Determine to be the best you can be in your area of effort. The athletes call it their P.B. - their personal best. If you are a mechanic - be the best. If you are a doctor - be the best. If you are a carpenter - be the best. A nurse - be the best. At a high school one time I asked a young man what he wanted to be. "A journalist" was his reply. I said, "Why not become the best journalist our country has ever seen?" Commit yourself. Give it your best, all you've got. Learn to love the word Discipline.

When you think you have given it all you have got, remember: your best can always be made better.

DO A LITTLE MORE
THAN YOU'RE PAID TO;
GIVE A LITTLE MORE
THAN YOU HAVE TO;
TRY A LITTLE HARDER
THAN YOU WANT TO;
AIM A LITTLE HIGHER
THAN YOU THINK POSSIBLE;
AND GIVE A LOT OF THANKS
TO GOD FOR HEALTH,
FAMILY AND FRIENDS.
'Art Linkletter'

Here then are the steps to become a person of action:-

1. **Be a goal setter**
2. **Be a self starter**
3. **Give it all you've got**
4. **Act now**

ASK YOURSELF CONSTANTLY - HOW CAN I DO IT BETTER?

Key
8

Do More Than Expected

GO THE SECOND MILE

Key
8

Do More Than Expected

Excellence is a powerful word. Everyone loves excellence and shuns mediocrity. And so they should.

People, companies or nations who do not set high standards will soon be left behind in a world of accelerating change and improvement.

Excellence is not achieved by accident. What we aim at determines what we will become, and while we may not always make our goals, our goals will always make us. To aim at excellence is to point your life towards the realisation of your potential, to endeavour to fulfil your capabilities.

1. THE MARKS OF A LIFE OF EXCELLENCE

A life of excellence demonstrates:-

a) the Mark of Productivity
All the meditation in the world has never produced a field of rice or wheat. "If a man will not work, he shall not eat," said the wise Paul. He also said - "Do not live unproductive lives."
The future arrives hour by hour. Seize every moment.

b) The Mark of Progress
A rut is just a grave with the ends opened out. Stagnant water is useless. So, too, is a life not given to progress.

c) The Mark of Power
When you have direction in life, you can harness your energies and produce power.

The great violinist Isaac Stern was once asked by a reporter, "What truly distinguishes a great musician?" Stern's reply was perceptive. "A great musician is one who is always seeking to improve, never content with his performances, always moving on to discover more about the instrument and the music he loves." That is excellence.

2. THE STANDARD OF EXCELLENCE

Each one of us is horrified at the poor products and service we receive today. No wonder there is a move to improve the standards. To have real value, excellence must encompass all areas of our life. A man may have an excellent business but his home and family are in chaos. An athlete may be a public hero and a private failure. Excellence must integrate our total life.

Saterman and Peters in their brilliant book, 'In Search of Excellence' studies The world's top companies for the secrets of their success. They report that, 'every excellent company is clear on what it stands for, and takes the process of value-shaping seriously'. 'They require and demand extraordinary performance for the ordinary man'. They suggest such companies have seven basic values.

1. A belief in being the "best".

2. A belief in the importance of the details of execution, the nuts and bolts of doing the job well.

3. A belief in the importance of people as individuals.

4. A belief in superior quality and service.

5. A belief that most members of the organisation should be innovators.

6. A belief in the importance of informality to enhance communication.

7. Explicit belief, in and recognition of, the importance of economic growth and profits.
(In Search of Excellence - New York, Harper & Row)

DUTY DETERMINES DESTINY

3. BECOME AMBITIOUS FOR EXCELLENCE

Without ambition, mediocrity is inevitable. What are your ambitions in life? What people achieve in their work and career depends greatly on their motivation, attitudes and values. Be a winner. Go the second mile. Go for the gold.

**THE DIFFERENCE BETWEEN
GOOD AND GREAT
IS A
LITTLE EXTRA EFFORT**

4. EXCELLENCE REQUIRES:

a) Risk. You will never discover new horizons without leaving the safety of the harbour.

b) Withstanding Criticism.

c) Responsibility - Not Capability (Remember, it's not I.Q. but I will)

d) Service and Work Brings Reward.

Excellence is the maximum exercise of one's gifts and abilities within the range of responsibilities you possess.

5. THE DANGERS OF EXCELLENCE

REMEMBER -
WHEN SUCCESS COMES YOUR WAY,
WALK IN HUMILITY

A mother whale once warned her son, "Remember, it's when you go to the top and start blowing that you get harpooned."

6. EXCELLENCE COSTS

a) The cost of changed values. Become an eagle to soar in the heavens. Don't be a chicken scratching in the dirt.

b) The cost of concentration. Don't dissipate your energies in all directions. If you zig-zag all your life, you won't reach your full potential.

c) The cost of continuation. Stickability sets the leader apart. There are so many people who are always going to get ready to begin, to prepare to start thinking about beginning one day to perhaps commence!

7. EXCELLENCE REQUIRES:

a) *Responsibility*
Be a catalyst, not a chameleon.

b) *Integrity*
Have character as a pacesetter and leader. There are too many power-holders today and not enough leaders.

c) *Industry*
Dream dreams, but pay the price of hard work to make them come true.

d) *Vision*
Don't be satisfied with the status quo.

e) *Creativity*
Have fixed principles in a flexible form. Be on the lookout constantly for fresh and new ideas.

f) *Unity*
Work with a team. "One shall put a thousand to flight but two shall put ten thousand to flight," says the scriptures.

g) *Strategy*
Determine priorities and develop procedures.

Aristotle said, "We are what we repeatedly do." Excellence then, is not an act but a habit. We must resist every situation that allows the good to be the enemy of the best. The wise Solomon stated, "Whatever your hand finds to do, do it with all your might." So many have great gifts, but are too lazy to unwrap them.

Dr David McClelland who is professor of psychology at Harvard University says, "It seems that most people in the world, psychologically, can be divided into two groups. There is the minority who are challenged by opportunity and willing to work hard to achieve something. On the other hand there is the majority who really don't care all that much."

Today we must stress excellence over mediocrity.

SOME MEN DIE IN ASHES
SOME MEN DIE IN FLAMES
SOME MEN DIE INCH BY INCH
PLAYING LITTLE CHILDREN'S GAMES.

The difference between good and great is a little extra effort.

SO - GO FOR THE GOLD

8. EXCELLENCE REQUIRES QUALITY

It may be quality in management, products or lifestyle. True success demands quality. The day of junk presentation is over. Study any winner. It is not their cleverness, but the fact that each and every aspect of their business, life or performance is just a touch better than the norm. Don't try to be one thousand percent better at one thing. Be one percent better at one thousand things.

As valuable as they may be, computers can tell you so much but it is only the human being that can really tell quality, in a product or performance.

Don't make the mistake of running a business or organisation on figures and finance alone or you will go under. Quality is the key to everything in our nation today.

EXCELLENCE DEMANDS QUALITY IN LEADERSHIP, PRODUCTS AND PERFORMANCE

Key
9

KEEP AT IT

IT'S ALWAYS TOO SOON
TO QUIT

Key
9

KEEP AT IT

Failure is only final if you let it be. The key is to learn from our failures. The man who has never made a mistake has never made anything. Learn to say "I'm down, but not out."

IT'S NOT WHETHER YOU GET KNOCKED DOWN, IT'S WHETHER YOU GET UP AGAIN.
- Vincent Lombardi

Here are a few things to remember concerning failure.

1. *To fail is not to be a failure.*
   At least you have tried. Remember, winning isn't always being first.

2. *Once you have learned from your failures, forget them.*
   If you brood over your failures, you will remember nothing else. Failure is no disgrace. If it were, we would all be disgraceful, Listen - I've never made a small mistake in my life!

3. *You are never a failure as long as you keep trying.*
   Better to fail attempting great deeds than to attempt nothing and succeed.

4. *Failure is never final - unless you allow it to be*.
   The choice is with you. You can either play it safe or get up and fight another round.

Edison failed at his first 6,000 attempts to develop a light bulb. When asked if he was discouraged, he replied, "No, I am now well informed on 6,000 ways you cannot do it."

The greatest failure in life is to stop trying.

Maybe you have tried to get a job many times. Get up, brush the dust off and go again. Perhaps your business is down, stand back and review and go again.

It is always too soon to quit. Never give up. Persist.

MEN NEVER PLAN TO BE FAILURES; THEY SIMPLY FAIL TO PLAN TO BE SUCCESSFUL.
-William A. Ward

Remember, dishonest success is a low form of failure. No man is a complete failure until he begins disliking men who succeed.

As one door closes look for another that is open. So often we look with such regret at the closed door that we do not see the one that is open before us. Defeat is nothing but education; it is the first step towards something better.

A traveller in Africa saw one of the large butterflies of the tropics struggling to free itself from the cocoon. He pitied it and with his knife, cut the cords at which it was straining. It was released, but all the brilliant colouring was gone! The struggle was necessary to make the colour appear. As you gain the victory over trial and adversity, you will see beautiful colours and qualities comes from your life. People that have never had difficulties or problems tend to be very shallow.

Great trials are often necessary to prepare us for great responsibilities. The longer you dwell on your misfortunes, the greater is their power to control you. No diamond or gem has ever been polished without friction. It is the irritation in the oyster that produces the pearl. The problems, difficulties and setbacks we have in life are all required for our development.

Regardless of how careful your planning may be, it is possible that your goal plan will not work perfectly. If the overall problem is too hard - break it up. Divide and conquer.

NEVER GIVE UP.
IT'S ALWAYS TOO SOON TO QUIT

REMEMBER:-

The five "D's" to success
Desire
Determination
Dedication
Discipline
Drive
The sixth "D" - Distraction
- to be avoided at all costs.

Sir Winston Churchill, during one of his many visits to his old school at Harrow, addressed the students in the following way. He was in a big dining hall that affords a view of the lights of London from Harrow on the Hill. The headmaster introduced the five foot five, 235 pound intellectual giant, in a flourishing manner. After graciously acknowledging the profuse introduction, Churchill made that never-to-be-forgotten statement, 'Young gentlemen, never give up, never give up, never give up, never, never, never, never.' And he sat down.

No better advice could be given to the potential leadership of the country.

It is always too soon to quit. I don't know what mountain you have to climb, what the burden is you have to carry, what problems you are facing, what trials and difficulties are surrounding you. But I know this - it is too soon to quit - never give up.

Success consists of getting up just one more time than you fall. It is like the postage stamp: its usefulness consists in the ability to stick to one thing until it gets there.

On his voyage to discover America, as day after day no land appeared, and again and again his sailors threatened mutiny and tried to persuade him to turn back, Columbus refused to listen to their entreaties and entered each day in the ship's log-book the two words - 'Sailed on!'

No man has ever exhausted the power that lies in the words, 'GO ON.

An executive at one time was taken down a peg. "You may well feel proud of yourself, young fellow," he said to the life insurance agent. "I've refused to see seven insurance men today." "I know," said the agent, "I'm them".

QUITTERS NEVER WIN AND WINNERS NEVER QUIT

Key
10

BE COMMITTED

YOU WILL NEVER
REALLY ACHIEVE IN LIFE
UNLESS YOU ARE
TOTALLY COMMITTED.

Key
10

Be Committed

A trend that I notice today is that no one really wants to be committed to anything. They don't want to sign on the dotted line. Nothing is going to happen for you when you are not willing to totally commit yourself to it.

Study any achiever or any person who has made a mark in our world. Not one of them vacillated in their commitment.

I see so many young people sitting around staring at their navel saying "Who am I?" They have their feet firmly planted in mid-air. They are like the politician when asked what his opinion was on a certain subject. He replied

"Well, some of my friends are for it and some of my friends are against it and I am for my friends!!" No commitment.

It is like an onion. If you peel one skin off then what do you have? Another skin. Peel off another or another until finally what is left - nothing! It is exactly the same for those trying to look within themselves to find themselves.

Show me what you are committed to and I will tell you who you are.

What are your dreams? Commit yourself to them with everything you are and have.

So many sit back, wishing. I saw people throwing coins into a wishing well, wishing for something to come true. The old saying is so true - "If it is to be - it's up to me."

STOP WISHING.
DREAM BIG DREAMS.
PLAN BIG PLANS.
MAKE GREAT COMMITMENTS.

Attempting something so great that it is doomed to failure unless you are totally committed to it.

People today are tip-toeing quietly to the grave!

Bill Faqua has the world's record for doing absolutely nothing. He is one of those people who stand in shopping centres, hours on end, motionless, not moving a muscle, doing nothing but amusing the crowd. I feel there are many today that could beat Bill Faqua's record. Because of their lack of commitment, their lives count for very little, not only for themselves but for their fellow man.

It is always better to fail in doing something than to excel in doing nothing.

OPPORTUNITY IS MISSED BY MOST PEOPLE BECAUSE IT IS DRESSED IN OVERALLS AND LOOKS LIKE WORK.
Thomas Edison

The secret of success is to start from scratch and keep on scratching. Don't ask, "What if it doesn't work?" Ask instead, "What if it does?" Of course there are difficulties and obstacles in life. No one is immune to problems. Even the lion has to fight off flies!

There are a lot of ways to become a failure, but never taking a chance is the most successful. Trials and troubles are a very real part of life.

IN THE PRESENCE OF TROUBLE SOME PEOPLE GROW WINGS, OTHERS BUY CRUTCHES.
Harold W Ruoff

You are an original - not a copy. You are unique - a one-off, never to be repeated. Life with all its incredible opportunities lies before you. Don't be defeated by others or yourself. You only have one life - one shot at it. Don't miss it, don't blow it. It is too valuable. So you have hit the dust. Get up, brush the dust off, get going again. Do it now. Seize the moment. Go for it.

Be like the steam kettle! Though it is up to its neck in hot water, it continues to sing! If you are complaining about the way the ball bounces, you may have been the one who dropped it. Don't say die until you're dead. So many think that opportunity means a chance to get money without earning it. Those who don't take chances don't make advances.

Keep on hanging in there with undaunted persistence. Winston Churchill said, "The nose of the bulldog is slanted backwards so he can continue to breathe without letting go." I had the privilege of walking through the old War Cabinet rooms in London still left exactly as they were during the second world war. Tenaciously he hung on with defeat looming on every hand, courageously undaunted he led the British along with the allies to victory.

It is not what you have but what you do with what you have that makes all the difference.

If it is necessary, get mad with yourself or the situation you are in, or the condition of your society. Most winners are just losers who got mad. You are like a tea bag - not much use until you've been through some hot water.

The wonderful blind lady Helen Keller said, "I am only one, but still I am one. I cannot do everything, but still I can do something. I will not refuse to do the something I can do".

Stop being satisfied with your life and achievements.

SHOW ME A THOROUGHLY SATISFIED MAN, AND I WILL SHOW YOU A FAILURE.
Thomas Edison

There is no telling what you can achieve in life if you are totally committed.

You will always be criticised. If you are in the front line you will be the first to be shot at. The only way to fend off criticism is to do nothing and be nothing. Those who do things inevitably stir up criticism. Go down to any park and see if there are any statues erected to a critic. If people talk negatively about you, live so that no one will believe them.

You cannot stay motivated for a dream in which you do not passionately believe. Commit yourself to your dream. See yourself in possession of it. Do all that it takes to become the person you need to be.

YOU CAN'T CONSISTENTLY PERFORM IN A MANNER THAT IS INCONSISTENT WITH THE WAY YOU SEE YOURSELF.
Zig Ziglar

Get going. Everything big starts with something little. No one ever stumbled on to something big while sitting down.

"Yes" and "No" are the two most important words you will ever say. These are the two words that determine your destiny in life. Say yes to commitment. Say yes to your dreams. Say yes to a positive future. Say yes to your goals.

LIFE IS EITHER A
DARING ADVENTURE OR NOTHING.
Helen Keller

You will never discover new oceans unless you have the courage to lose sight of the shore.

You can't walk backward into the future.

Face it.

Commit yourself to it.

Go for it.

EPILOGUE

YOUR GAME PLAN TO GET GOING

All of the encouragement in this book is useless unless you determine to establish a plan of action. Let me suggest some positive ideas to get you started.

1. Clearly define where you are at this moment. So much time is wasted by unclear thinking. Clear thinking is vital and needed. Evaluate your life and set some priorities.

2. Take time aside in a quiet place to be alone. Start dreaming dreams as to the kind of life you want to live. Write down a plan of action, putting on paper all that comes to your mind.

3. List any obstacles that may be in your way) e.g. lack of education, health etc.).

4. Write down the steps you will be willing to take to overcome those obstacles (e.g. special courses etc.). Make your plan workable and practical.

5. Make a realistic estimate of time needed to achieve this - set deadlines.

6. Nothing will happen unless you develop a burning desire to achieve results. Do not be wishy-washy. Wishing will not make it happen. Replace vague hopes with a deep sincere desire.

7. Constantly re evaluate your goals. Spend time often quietly over them again and again.

8. Do not allow yourself to get side tracked. Forget what others say, think or do.

9. Carry yourself like the person you desire to become ("As a man thinks in his heart, so is he").

Our nation is crying out for leaders and achievers. Your life is filled with destiny, meaning and purpose. My prayer for you is that you will discover:

- "The Power of a Successful Life."

POWER POINTS

Remember

PEOPLE BECOME WHAT THEY THINK ABOUT

- If you do not control your thought life, you will be a slave to your surroundings.
- If you want to be successful, you must think until it hurts.
- Take time to think - it is the source of power.
- Today is the tomorrow you worried about yesterday.
- Don't let the dissenters be the deciders.
- Throw the thought poison out of your environment.
- As a man thinks in his heart - so is he.

ARE YOU KICKING AT GOALS OR JUST KEEPING SCORE?

- Opportunities never come to those who wait. They are captured by those who dare to attach.
- Henry Kaiser said "Determine what you want more than anything else in life, write down the means by which you intend to attain it, and permit nothing to deter you from pursuing it.

DO IT NOW

- There is no gain without pain.
- Losers let it happen - Winners make it happen.
- It takes little size to criticise
- Develop an above average handshake.
- The sweetest word in the English language is a person's name.
- The truest test of a person's character is what they are like when they are alone.
- Without real friends, even a millionaire is poor.
- Think enthusiastically.
- Be yourself but be your best self.
- I have nothing to prove - just someone to please.
- You have only one chance at a good first impression.
- This one thing I do, not those hundred things I dabble at.
- What you don't use - you lose.
- Not what can I get but what can I give.
- The most important letter in the alphabet is the letter "W" - it changes a "No" to a "Now".

WORDS CONDITION YOUR THINKING AND OTHERS SO TALK POSITIVELY

- All of us have formulated a mental image of ourselves based on the feelings of acceptance we received from our parents.
- What you say is what you are.

**DON'T NURSE YOUR HURTS,
DON'T REHEARSE YOUR HURTS,
DON'T CURSE HURTS
BUT REVERSE YOUR HURTS
BECAUSE HURTS WILL MAKE YOU
BITTER OR BETTER**

- Turn the problem into a propeller.
- If you are in the front line you are the first to get shot at.

YOU GO LIKE THE COMPANY YOU KEEP

- If you want friends in life, you must show yourself to be friendly.
- Friendship is the inexpressible comfort of feeling safe with a person, having neither to weigh thoughts nor measure the words.
- My best friend is the one who brings out the best in me.

THE KEY TO SUCCESS IS ATTENTION TO DETAIL

- This world does not owe you a living you have to get out there and make a living.
- The only place were success comes before work is in the dictionary.

GO THE SECOND MILE

- Duty determines destiny.
- The difference between good and great is a little extra effort.
- Remember - When success comes your way, walk in humility.
- Some men die in ashes,
  Some men die in flames,
  Some men die inch by inch,
  Playing little children's games.
- So - Go for the gold.
- Excellence demands quality in leadership, product and performance.
- Do a little more than you're paid to;
  Give a little more than you have to;
  Try a little harder than you want to;
  Aim a little higher than you think possible;
  And give a lot of thanks to God for health, family and friends.

- Think - How can I do it better.

IT'S ALWAYS TOO SOON TO QUIT

- It's not whether you get knocked down, it's whether you get up again.
- Men never have to be failures; they simply fail to be successful.
- Never give up, it's always too soon to quit.
- Quitters never win and winners never quit.
- The five "D's" to success - Desire, Determination, Dedication, Discipline, Drive - the sixth "D" Distraction - to be avoided at all costs.

BE COMMITTED

- You will never really achieve in life unless you are totally committed.

- Stop wishing. Dream big dreams Plan big plans. Make great commitments.

- Opportunity is missed by most people because it is dressed in overalls and looks like work.

- In the presence of trouble some people grow wings, others buy crutches.

- Show me a thoroughly satisfied man, and I will show you a failure.

- You can't consistently perform in a manner that is inconsistent with the way you see yourself.

- Life is either a daring adventure or nothing.

PUBLICATIONS BY THE SAME AUTHOR

HOW TO AVOID DETOURS ON THE ROAD TO SUCCESS

Very often we are our own worst enemy. The Road to Success contains keys to help you conquer the ten most common causes of failure such as Having the Wrong Goals; Quitting Too Soon; Burdens of the Past.

THE TEN LAWS OF LEADERSHIP

Just as there are principles that govern nature, so there are definite principles which are vital in leadership. Don't stagger on in ignorance. Study well these principles to become the leader you are meant to be.

SOARING WITH EAGLES

Eagles are magnificent creatures. Since ancient times many have used the eagle as their symbol. These principles of success are vital to us all. Allow the monarch of the skies, the eagle, to teach you how your life can count.

FAMILY LIFE IN THE FAST LANE

The needs of families have never been greater than today. Bill Newman gives you some sensible keys for strengthening and enriching marriage and family life.